"Now will you come into the warm, Eric?" asked Surf.

People came from far and wide to visit the little rock-pool garden ...

So he made a wooden sign to put beside his pool,
and wrote on it 'In memory of you. I miss you dreadfully.'

Surf looked at the rock pool with all its flowers.
"Oh, it's lovely," she said, "like a little sea."

This pleased Eric very much.

Yet he suddenly knew that his memories of the sea were like a special kind of treasure in his mind.

A treasure he had not lost. A treasure no one could take away from him. A treasure he would keep very safe inside his heart.

And as he spoke,
tears rolled down his cheeks.

"I remember," he began. "I remember her swirling and her swooshing, and her beautiful fish, and the shells she brought me when she came from far away."

Then Surf gave Eric a special-looking shell.
"Put this to your ear," she said. And when Eric did, he heard the sea, his lovely sea. Yes, that was her sound alright, that was her sound.

And he told Surf all about his lovely sea.

"I am very lost," sobbed Eric.

But after he let Surf comfort him, the sun peeped out from behind the clouds for the first time in ages.

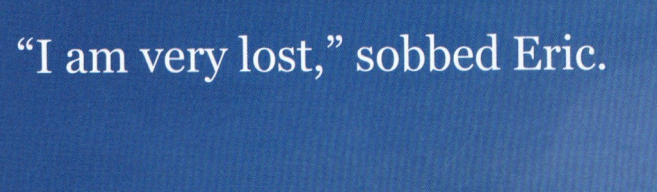

But after all the digging and the building, Eric started to cry. "How brave of you to cry," said Surf, "because it really hurts to feel how much you miss someone who's gone. Yet those who dare not feel their pain, can close their hearts and never truly love again."

And so that the flowers could always have water, Surf helped Eric to make a rock pool.

... and another, and another,
        until many flowers had pushed themselves up through the hard, hard rocks on the sand.

And then another little flower popped up,

so he watered that ...

"Thank you, thank you!" said the little flower as it drank the water with glee.

Eric took it, and ran back as fast as he could to the little flower.

After a while, he came across a wise old dog called Surf.
Surf gave Eric her drinking bowl of water.

So Eric ran and ran along the beach as fast as he could, to see if he could find water.

"There is no water here," said Eric.

At that the flower looked terribly sad, and started to droop very badly.

Eric felt a rush of fear, "Don't die. Please don't die. I will find water."

Then one day, pushing up through a tiny crack in that hard, hard rock in front of him, came a little wild flower.

"How did you push up through all that hard, hard rock?" asked Eric.
"Dunno," said the little flower, "I just felt it was worth it.
But now I am so thirsty."

Then he felt the sting of his terrible sadness.

"I don't want to feel anything ever again," he said. "Why can't I forget? Why can't I be like rock, or stone – all frozen and still inside?"

Some days it rained sand, there was no water.
His friends brought him blankets and hot chocolate,
but he was too sad to take them.
The sea had taken everything lovely in its going, and
it seemed to Eric as if deadness might take over completely.

And although it was summer, winter came that day.
The ground froze, yet still Eric lay there.
The wind was biting, the air was bitterly cold.

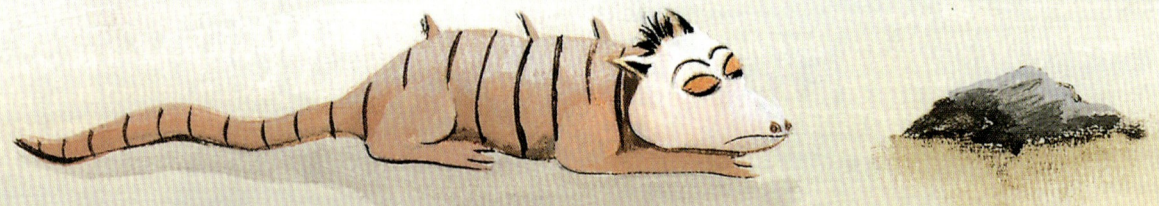

Yet still he lay there.

But after a while, Eric knew the terrible truth.
The sea was gone.
The awful thing had happened, and no one had stopped it.

So he fell on the sand and cried.

"Don't leave me. Please don't leave me," he sobbed,

"you are my everything."

He looked out at the cold, cold nothing and called, "Please, please come back."

He screwed his eyes tight to try and find the sea
on the dim horizon;
he could not.

Eric waited and waited, but it didn't come back.

But one day, the sea went out, and it didn't come back.

Sometimes he sat on a big rock, laughing with joy as the waves rushed over his feet.

Every day Eric played by the sea.
Sometimes he made a sandcastle with a lovely moat
for the sea to flow into.
Sometimes he sailed his little paper boats.

"Goodbye, goodbye!" he said, when it went out again, "See you soon!"

And he did.

"Hello, hello!" he said, when it moved towards him.

And as if the sea heard Eric, it gave an extra strong and swooshing sound.

... and coming back.

Once, there was a sand dragon called Eric.
Eric loved the sea very, very much.
Each day he watched it going out ...

Cover image: Nicky Armstrong.

Second edition published 2022
by Routledge
4 Park Square, Milton Park, Abingdon, Oxon, OX14 4RN

and by Routledge
605 Third Avenue, New York, NY 10158

Routledge is an imprint of the Taylor & Francis Group, an informa business

© 2022 Margot Sunderland and Nicky Armstrong

The right of Margot Sunderland to be identified as author of this work and Nicky Armstrong to be identified as illustrator of this work has been asserted in accordance with sections 77 and 78 of the Copyright, Designs and Patents Act 1988.

All rights reserved. No part of this book may be reprinted or reproduced or utilised in any form or by any electronic, mechanical, or other means, now known or hereafter invented, including photocopying and recording, or in any information storage or retrieval system, without permission in writing from the publishers.

Trademark notice: Product or corporate names may be trademarks or registered trademarks, and are used only for identification and explanation without intent to infringe.

First edition published by Speechmark 2003

British Library Cataloguing-in-Publication Data
A catalogue record for this book is available from the British Library

Library of Congress Cataloging-in-Publication Data
A catalog record for this book has been requested

ISBN: 978-1-032-10193-4 (pbk)
ISBN: 978-1-003-21412-0 (ebk)

DOI: 10.4324/9781003214120

Typeset in Georgia
by Apex CoVantage, LLC

The Day the Sea Went Out and Never Came Back

A Story for Children Who Have Lost Someone They Love

Second Edition

Margot Sunderland   Illustrated by **Nicky Armstrong**

Routledge
Taylor & Francis Group

LONDON AND NEW YORK

Helping Children with Feelings

Margot Sunderland's bestselling series of therapeutic stories for children, each accompanied by a professional guidebook, is designed to help children aged 4-12 connect with unresolved feelings affecting their behaviour.

Using Story Telling as a Therapeutic Tool with Children

Helping Children with Loss: A Guidebook (2e)
The Day the Sea Went Out and Never Came Back: A Story for Children Who Have Lost Someone They Love (2e)

Helping Children Pursue Their Hopes and Dreams: A Guidebook
A Pea Called Mildred: A Story to Help Children Pursue Their Hopes and Dreams

Helping Children who Bottle Up Their Feelings: A Guidebook
A Nifflnoo Called Nevermind: A Story for Children who Bottle Up Their Feelings

Helping Children who have Hardened Their Hearts or Become Bullies: A Guidebook
A Wibble Called Bipley: A Story for Children who have Hardened Their Hearts or Become Bullies

Helping Children who are Anxious or Obsessional: A Guidebook
Willy and the Wobbly House: A Story for Children who are Anxious and Obsessional

Helping Children Who Yearn for Someone They Love: A Guidebook
The Frog Who Longed for the Moon to Smile: A Story for Children who Yearn for Someone They Love

Helping Children Locked in Rage or Hate: A Guidebook
How Hattie Hated Kindness: A Story for Children Locked in Rage or Hate

Helping Children with Fear: A Guidebook
Teenie Weenie in a Too Big World: A Story for Fearful Children

Helping Children with Low Self-Esteem: A Guidebook
Ruby and the Rubbish Bin: A Story for Children with Low Self-Esteem

Helping Children of Troubled Parents: A Guidebook
Monica Plum's Horrid Problem: A Story for Children of Troubled Parents

The Day the Sea Went Out and Never Came Back

Eric is a sand dragon who loves the sea very much. Each day, he watches it go out, knowing that it will return. But one day, Eric waits and waits, but it does not come back. He falls on the sand, feeling as if he has lost everything. Eric wants to shut himself off from his feelings, but eventually spots a little wild flower growing, and another, and another. He builds a rock-pool garden, in memory of the sea that he loves, and learns that it is much better to feel the full pain of his loss, instead of closing his heart.

The Day the Sea Went Out and Never Came Back is a story for children who have lost someone they love. The beautiful illustrations and sensitively written story offer a wealth of opportunities to begin a conversation about the difficult emotions that can follow a loss, helping children to acknowledge and express their emotions. The story shows them that it is brave to feel sad, that they are surrounded by support, and that memories of a loved one are a special treasure that can never be lost.

Ideal for starting conversations about grief and sadness, this is an essential resource for anybody supporting children aged 4–12 who have experienced loss.

Margot Sunderland is Director of Education and Training at The Centre for Child Mental Health London, Co-Director of Trauma Informed Schools UK, Honorary Visiting Fellow at London Metropolitan University, Senior Associate Member of the Royal College of Medicine, and Child Psychotherapist with over thirty years' experience of working with children, teenagers (many in residential care homes) and families. She is also a qualified secondary school teacher.

Margot is author of over twenty books in the field of child mental health, which collectively have been translated into eighteen languages and published in twenty-four countries. Her internationally acclaimed book, *The Science of Parenting* won a first prize in the British Medical Association Medical Book awards and has been voted as one of the best brain books of our time by The Dana Foundation. Dr Sunderland has been studying the neuroscience of adult-child relationships for seventeen years. Dr Sunderland is also founding Director of The Institute for Arts in Therapy and Education, a Higher Education College and Academic Partner of University of East London. The College runs master's degrees/diplomas in Child Psychotherapy, Child Counselling, Parent-Child Therapy and Therapeutic Play.

Nicky Armstrong holds an MA from the Slade School of Fine Art and a BA Hons in Theatre Design from the University of Central England. She has illustrated over thirty-four books in the mental health field, which have been translated into five languages/countries. She works full time as an illustrator and fine artist. She has achieved major commissions nationally and internationally in mural work and fine art.